ANNE ROCKWELL

I FLY

illustrated by ANNETTE CABLE

Dragonfly Books™ Crown Publishers, Inc., New York

For Nicholas, who took his first plane ride with me
—A. R.

To the one I fly with, M. C. —Love, A. C.

DRAGONFLY BOOKS™ PUBLISHED BY CROWN PUBLISHERS, INC.

Text copyright © 1997 by Anne Rockwell
Illustrations copyright © 1997 by Annette Cable
All rights reserved. No part of this book may be reproduced or transmitted in any form or by any means,
electronic or mechanical, including photocopying, recording, or by any information storage and retrieval system,
without permission in writing from the publisher.

Published by Crown Publishers, Inc., a Random House company, 201 East 50th Street, New York, NY 10022

CROWN is a trademark of Crown Publishers, Inc.
http://www.randomhouse.com/

Library of Congress Cataloging-in-Publication Data
Rockwell, Anne F.
I fly / by Anne Rockwell ; illustrated by Annette Cable.
p.   cm.
Summary: A child describes his airplane trip to visit his cousins.
[1. Flight—Fiction. 2. Airplanes—Fiction.] I. Title.
PZ7.R5943Iaf   1997
[E]—dc20   94-29278

ISBN   0-517-59683-0 (trade)
0-517-59684-9 (lib. bdg.)
0-517-88569-7 (pbk.)

First Dragonfly Books™ edition: June 1998

Printed in Singapore
10 9 8 7 6 5 4 3 2 1

When I visit my cousins, I fly.
At the end of the tunnel that leads to the plane,
I pass the cockpit, where the pilot and co-pilot sit.
The pilot is the captain of the plane.

My seat is by the window right over the wing.

I like to look out the window when I fly.

The big jet plane is bumpy and clumsy as it rolls along the ground.

I watch the flaps go up on the wing outside.

The seat belt light turns on. A buzzer sounds, and I fasten my seat belt.

A flight attendant gives us safety instructions.

Then the pilot greets us over the speaker system.
"This is Captain Joseph Ramirez," he says.
"Welcome aboard Flight 234.
We are cleared for takeoff shortly.
Our flying time is one hour and twenty minutes.
I hope you enjoy your flight."

Jet engines begin to roar.
The sound grows louder and louder.
Our plane starts down the runway—
fast, then faster, faster, faster!
Then I feel it.
I feel the big plane lift off the ground, into the air.
I feel it in my stomach first, and then in my ears.

Up we go.
Now I am flying!
I hear the landing gear come up.
We don't need wheels up in the sky.

As the plane goes higher,
the sound of the engines
becomes a high-pitched whine.
I watch the silver wing
tilt downward,
and the world tips up to me.
The plane is banking.
That's how it turns,
up here in the sky. I like it.
It's sort of like the rides at
the fair, but better.
The city below grows smaller.
Tiny boats with little
white wakes
are scattered around
the harbor.

"To the right there's a great view
of the city skyline," the captain says.

I can see it if I press my nose to the window,
but all of a sudden we're inside a cloud,
and then it's gone.

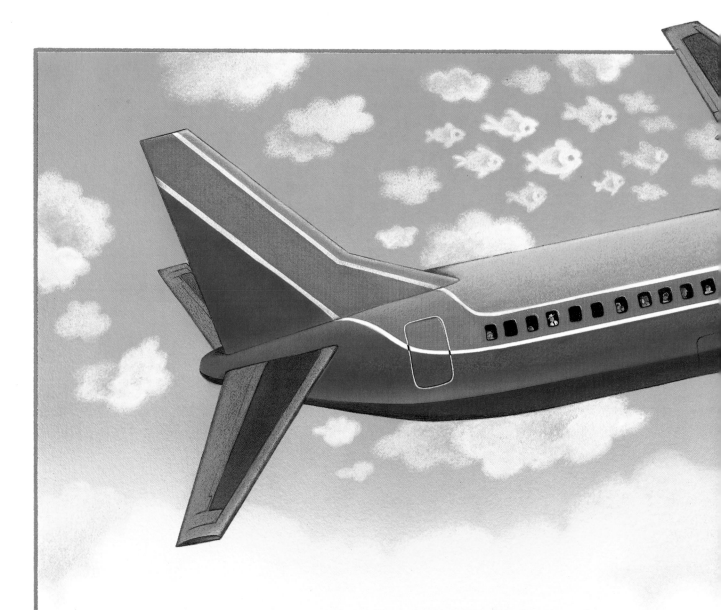

The plane keeps going up, up, up.
My ears pop.
I yawn a big yawn to keep them from popping again.
When I am on the ground, I look up at the clouds in the sky.
But now that I am flying,

I look down on them far below me.

There are millions and millions of puffy white clouds.

The flaps on the wing are level now.

It seems like the silver plane is standing still,

way above the clouds, but it's really going very fast.

"This is your captain speaking," Captain Ramirez says.
"We have reached our cruising altitude of thirty-five thousand feet.
Our speed is five hundred and forty miles an hour."

The buzzer sounds, and the seat belt light goes off.
The flight attendants bring small bags of peanuts to eat
and juice or soda to drink.

Way up here in the blue sky,
I can see the curve of the world.
Five hundred and forty miles
an hour is fast.
No racing car can go this fast,
but I can.
And thirty-five thousand feet is
about seven miles.
No birds can fly this high,
but I can.

Suddenly there's a break in the clouds.
Down below, I see dark blue-and-green patches.
It looks like a map, but before I can read it,
fluffy clouds hide the ground again.

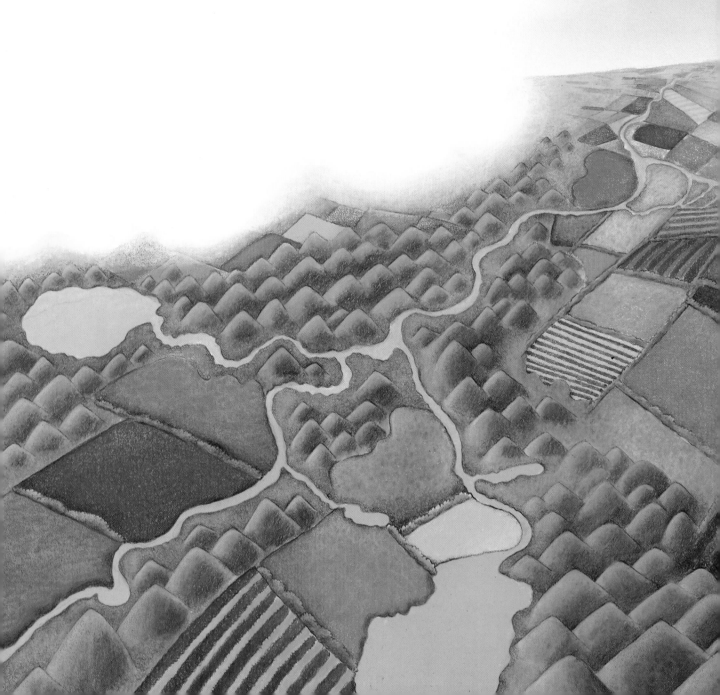

A flight attendant takes my
plastic cup away.
I fasten my tray to the
seat in front.
The seat belt light
goes on.

The buzzer sounds.
"We are beginning our
descent now,"
the captain says.
"The ground temperature is
eighty-two degrees.
The sun is shining.
Winds are north-northwest
at twelve miles an hour.
Visibility is ten miles—
a beautiful day."

Ragged streaks of cloud run past my window.
Wind makes the big plane shake.
The wings quiver, and suddenly we're inside a cloud again.
I'm glad my seat belt is fastened.

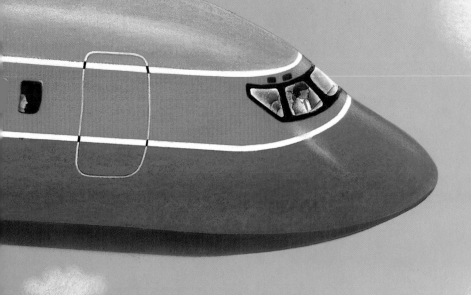

I think it must be exciting to be a pilot, or even a co-pilot.
It must be fun to make a big plane
go thirty-five thousand feet up into the sky
and then come down.

We zoom through the cloud.
The shadow of our plane moves over the land,
which looks like the quilt on my bed at home.
Silver ribbons crisscross squares of bright green and gold.

One wriggles alongside a dark green shape
that looks like the monster I know how to draw.
A shadow of cloud passes over the wing,
and the plane banks.

The silver ribbons
become roads and a river.
The green and gold squares
are fields,
and the dark green shape
is a range of hills.
Little cubes
that look like toy blocks
turn into barns and silos
and houses.
One is the house
where my aunt and uncle
and cousins live,
but I don't know which one.

I hear the landing gear clank down.
The flaps on the wing go straight up.
Suddenly the runway below
looks as though it's coming up to meet us,
we're going down so fast.
Down, down, down we fly.

And then, *bump! bump!*
The wheels hit the tarmac,
and we're not flying anymore.
Jet engines roar as they reverse.
We race down the long runway.
The wing flaps shake and tremble,
but stay up strong and straight.

I wonder if the plane is ever going to stop.
But then, before you know it,
it goes slower and slower and slower
until it has almost stopped.
The jet engines grow quiet.
We taxi slowly to the terminal.

The seat belt light goes off.

"Thank you for flying with us," Captain Ramirez says.

The big plane is still,

and all the people get up out of their seats.

When I step out the door of the plane,

I wave good-bye to our pilot and co-pilot, and they wave back.

I walk through the tunnel into the terminal.
And there they are—Aunt Sally and Uncle Ray,
Margie and Michael and little Jack.
They are all at the airport, waiting for me.
"Did you have a good flight?" Uncle Ray asks.
"I sure did," I say. "I love to fly."